Pam had a big dog.
His name was Duke.

Pam and Duke
ran home.

Jim had made a cake.
“I like cake,”
said Pam.

Pam ate the cake.
Duke did not get cake.

"It is time to ride my bike," said Pam.

Pam ran to get
her bike.

“I like cake,”
said Duke.

Duke hit the cake.
The cake fell.

The cake fell on top of Duke.

Pam came home.
The cake was
on the tile.

Jim came in.
"My cake is a mess!"
"The tile is a mess,"
said Pam.

“We can use the mop,”
said Pam.
“It will wipe up
the cake.”

Duke came to Jim
and Pam.
Duke was sad.
He had cake on
his nose.

"Cake on a dog is cute," said Jim.

Duke did not like cake
on him.
"I can use the hose
on Duke," said Jim.

Jim gave Duke a bone. Duke can have a bone, but he can not have cake.